Discover
Spain

Simon Rice

PowerKiDS press.

New York

Published in 2010 by The Rosen Publishing Group Inc.
29 East 21st Street, New York, NY 10010

First Edition

Concept design: Jason Billin
Editor: Paul Manning
Designer: Clare Nicholas
Consultant: Rob Bowden

Library of Congress Cataloging-in-Publication Data

Rice, Simon, 1957-
  Discover Spain / Simon Rice.
     p. cm. -- (Discover countries)
  Includes index.
  ISBN 978-1-61532-301-2 (library binding)
  ISBN 978-1-61532-302-9 (paperback)
  ISBN 978-1-61532-303-6 (6-pack)
  1. Spain--Juvenile literature. I. Title.
  DP17.R45 2010
  946--dc22
                              2009023725

Photographs:
1, 5, Shutterstock/Vinicius Tupinamba; 3t, Shutterstock/Shutterlist; 3b, EASI-Images/Ed Parker; 4 (map), Stefan Chabluk;
6, Shutterstock/Philip Lange; 7, Shutterstock/Ivan Montero Martinez; 8, Shutterstock/Marek Slusarczyk; 9, EASI-Images/
Chris Fairclough; 10, EASI-Images/Chris Fairclough; 11, Shutterstock/Nick Stubbs; 12, EASI-Images/Chris Fairclough;
13, EASI-Images/Chris Fairclough; 14, Corbis/Miguel Angel Molina; 15, Shutterstock/Katja Wickert; 16, Corbis/Emilio Naranjo;
17, Corbis/Jesus Diges; 18, Shutterstock/Rafael Ramirez Lee; 19, Corbis/JB Russel; 20, Corbis/Marco Cristofori;
21, Shutterstock/Albo; 22, EASI-Images/Chris Fairclough; 23, Shutterstock/Hannu Liivaar; 24, Shutterstock/Jose A.S. Reyes;
25, Shutterstock/Jarno Gonzalez Zarraonandia; 26, Shutterstock/Elena Grigorova; 27, Shutterstock/Vicente Barcelo Varona;
28, Shutterstock/NHTG; 29, Shutterstock/Martin Trajkovski.
Cover images: TK

Manufactured in China
CPSIA Compliance Information: Batch #WAW0102PK: For Further Information
contact Rosen Publishing, New York, New York at 1-800-237-9932

Contents

Discovering Spain

Spain is the second-largest country in Europe. It includes the Balearic Islands in the Mediterranean Sea, the Canary Islands in the Atlantic, and two cities, Ceuta and Melilla, in Morocco, North Africa. Since the 1960s, tourism has helped to make Spain one of Europe's wealthiest countries.

Spain and its neighbors

With its smaller neighbor Portugal, Spain occupies the Iberian Peninsula at the far western edge of Europe. In the north, it is separated from France by a chain of mountains called the Pyrenees. In the south, Spain is just 8 miles (13 km) from Africa across the Straits of Gibraltar.

Spain is made up of 17 regions that were once separate kingdoms. When North African Muslims called the Moors invaded Spain in 711 CE, the Spanish kingdoms gradually joined forces to defeat them. This period was known as the *Reconquista* or "reconquest" (722–1492). Afterward, the kingdoms united and in 1561, Madrid was chosen as the country's capital.

Spain Statistics

Capital city: Madrid

Government type: Constitutional monarchy

Bordering countries: Andorra, France, United Kingdom (Gibraltar), Portugal, Morocco (Ceuta), Morocco (Melilla)

Currency: Euro (€)

Languages: Castilian, Catalan (Catalonia), Euskara (Basque Country), Galego (Galicia)

Key
- ■ Capital city
- ● Other cities

Modern Spain

Between 1936 and 1939, a war was fought in Spain between republican and nationalist forces. After the defeat of the republicans, the nationalist leader, General Francisco Franco, took power and continued to rule the country until his death in 1975.

Today, Spain is a constitutional monarchy with a king, Juan Carlos I (1938–), as head of state. The country is run by a parliament called the Cortes. Its present prime minister is José Luis Rodríguez Zapatero.

Although Spain is governed from Madrid, each region has its own identity and its own parliament. Many regions would like to be more independent. In the Basque Country in northern Spain, there has been a long campaign of violence by extremists who want their region to be completely separate from Spain.

▲ The Plaza Mayor, or central square, of the Spanish capital, Madrid.

DID YOU KNOW? At 2,188 feet (667 meters) above sea level, Madrid is Europe's highest capital city. Situated in the geographical center of the country, it is also the only European capital not located on a major river.

Landscape and climate

Spain is a country of contrasting landscapes. A high, flat plateau known as the Meseta Central covers the central part of the country. This region is so dry that some of it is desert. At the opposite extreme, Spain's Atlantic coastline is green and fertile, and prone to storms and flooding.

⚠ Long periods of drought affect large areas of Spain's central plateau.

Mountains and rivers

Spain has an average altitude of 2,132 feet (650 meters) above sea level, making it the second most mountainous country in Europe after Switzerland. Some of its mountain ranges, or *sierras*, form chains around the coast, such as the Cordillera Cantabrica in the north and the Sierra Nevada in the south. Spain's largest mountain range is the Pyrenees.

Although much of Spain is dry, the Iberian Peninsula has several major rivers. The Ebro flows through Spain's central region, from Cantabria in the northwest to the Mediterranean Sea in the southeast. The Guadalquivir flows southwest through Andalusia to the Atlantic. At 645 miles (1,038 km), the longest river in the Iberian Peninsula is the Tagus, which flows through central Spain, then Portugal and into the Atlantic.

Facts at a glance

Land area: 192,874 sq. miles (499,542 sq. km)

Water area: 2,023 sq. miles (5,240 sq. km)

Highest point: Pico de Teide (Tenerife) on Canary Islands, 12,198 feet (3,718 m)

Coastline: 3,084 miles (4,964 km)

Longest river (Spain): Ebro, 565 miles (909 km)

Longest river (Iberian Peninsula): Tagus, 645 miles (1,038 km)

Spain's climates

Spain has three different types of climate. The northern coastal area has high rainfall and mild winters, but with strong gales. The south and east coasts have a Mediterranean climate, with hot, dry summers and cool, wet winters. The central region has a continental climate, with freezing winters, very hot summers, and dry conditions all year round.

Much of Spain suffers from droughts that can last for several years, but in the coastal mountains, heavy rain can cause serious flooding.

DID YOU KNOW?

Almond, orange, and olive trees are a feature of the Spanish countryside. The cork used in wine bottles comes from the bark of oak trees that grow on the open woodland of Spain's central plateau.

▼ The northern coastal area of Spain is often called "Green Spain," because of its mild, wet climate.

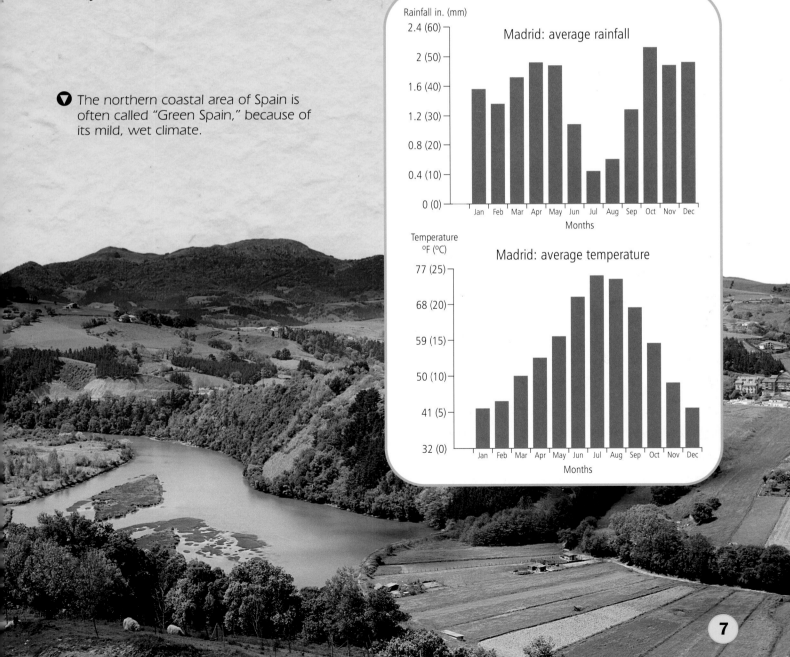

Rainfall in. (mm)

Madrid: average rainfall

Months

Temperature °F (°C)

Madrid: average temperature

Months

7

Population and health

Over the last century, Spain's population doubled to 46 million. Much of the growth took place in the 1960s and 1970s, when Spain's economy boomed as a result of the growth of tourism and industry. But in the 1980s, the birth rate fell dramatically as lifestyles changed and Spanish people began to have smaller families.

Life expectancy

During the first half of the twentieth century, most Spaniards lived in rural villages or towns where standards of health were often low. From the 1960s onward, many people moved to the cities, and government-funded healthcare became widely available for the first time. By the early 2000s, Spain had more doctors per member of the population than most other countries in the European Union (E.U.), and life expectancy in Spain was among the highest in the world.

Facts at a glance

Total population: 45.2 million

Life expectancy at birth:
77.2 years (male)
83.7 years (female)

Children dying before the age of five:
4 per 1,000 live births

Access to safe water: 100%

La Boqueria food market in Barcelona. Fresh fruit and vegetables are an important part of the Spanish diet and help to keep Spanish people fit and healthy.

DID YOU KNOW?
One reason why Spanish people live longer is that their diet includes large amounts of olive oil. Unlike animal fats, olive oil lowers cholesterol and blood pressure, reducing the risk of heart disease.

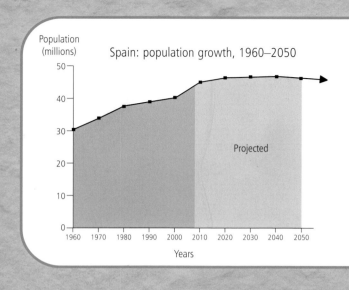

Population (millions)

Spain: population growth, 1960–2050

50

40

30

20

10

0

Projected

1960 1970 1980 1990 2000 2010 2020 2030 2040 2050

Years

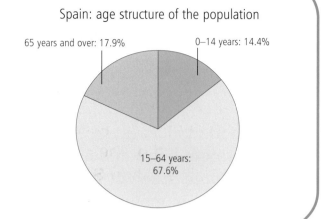

Spain: age structure of the population

65 years and over: 17.9%

0–14 years: 14.4%

15–64 years: 67.6%

Spain's aging population

Because people in Spain are living longer, the number of older people is increasing. In the future, it may be difficult for Spain to look after its growing numbers of older people, since there will be fewer workers paying the taxes needed to support senior citizens.

Immigration

Despite the falling birth rate, Spain's population has continued to grow since 2000. The main reason for this has been immigration. Over five million immigrants are registered as living in Spain, but illegal immigration could make that figure much higher.

The largest group of immigrants are from South America. Those who speak Spanish and whose skills are in demand can often enjoy opportunities that are not available in their country of origin. But not all immigrants adapt easily to life in Spain. Large numbers come from Africa, particularly Morocco. Most of these migrants do not speak Spanish when they arrive, and they often work in low-paid jobs.

⬥ Since 2000, large numbers of immigrants, including more than half a million from North Africa, have boosted Spain's population.

Settlements and living

Apart from Madrid, most of Spain's population is concentrated in urban centers around the coast, and large areas of the country are thinly populated. This is mostly due to people leaving rural areas to find work and better living conditions in the cities.

The drift to the cities

At different times over the last hundred years, large numbers of people have moved from the countryside to Spain's urban areas. During the late 1960s and early 1970s, sprawling suburbs grew up to house people seeking work in the booming industrial cities and tourist centers. The most rapid growth took place in the largest cities: Madrid, Barcelona, Valencia, Seville, Zaragoza, Malaga, and Murcia.

This growth occurred with very little planning. Many migrants to the cities could only find housing in cheaply built apartment buildings, often in areas where there were few stores, schools, or other local services.

> **Facts at a glance**
>
> **Average population density**:
> 227 per sq. mi (88 per sq. km)
>
> **Urban population**:
> 34.8 million
>
> **Rural population**:
> 10.4 million
>
> **Population of largest city**:
> 3.1 million (Madrid)

▶ Street life in a Catalonian town. Narrow, shady streets like this can be found in the center of many Spanish towns and cities.

Living in the city

In recent years, the drift to the cities has continued, and almost 80 percent of the population now live in urban areas. Most city dwellers live in apartment buildings five stories high.

Much of the worst housing of the 1960s and 1970s has now been rebuilt, and parks, leisure facilities, and other services have been provided. But many of Spain's large cities still suffer from overcrowding, traffic congestion, and pollution.

Moving to the suburbs

On the fringes of many Spanish cities, there are now new housing developments called *urbanisaciones*, which have communal gardens and swimming pools. Houses here are popular with young families, but they are expensive to buy, and cars are vital for access to work, stores, and leisure facilities.

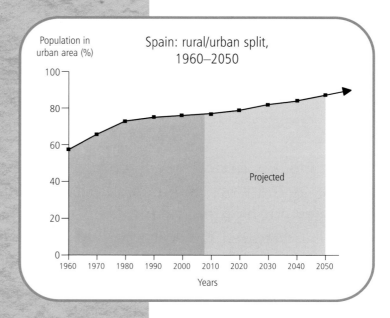

Population in urban area (%)

Spain: rural/urban split, 1960–2050

Projected

Years

DID YOU KNOW? The typical Andalusian village is a clutter of small, white houses and narrow streets. Long ago, the houses were bright-colored, but painting them white was thought to help resist the spread of plague.

◀ New-style suburban housing on the outskirts of Malaga.

Family life

Family life has always been important to Spanish people. In the past, young people lived at home until they got married, and three generations would often live together in the same house. In modern Spain, this traditional type of extended family lifestyle is becoming much less common.

The decline in marriage

Since 1980, the marriage rate in Spain has been falling. At the same time, the age at which people get married and start raising a family has generally been getting higher. Currently, the average age at which women get married is around 29, and men marry slightly later at around 31.

Families have also become smaller than in the past. Under Franco, when the influence of the Catholic Church was strong, Spanish people were encouraged to raise large families. But with the drift of population to towns and cities, lifestyles have changed, and families of more than three or four children are now rare.

Facts at a glance

Average children per childbearing woman:
1.3 children

Average household size:
2.9 people

▼ With more women working full-time, grandparents often play an important part in looking after young children in Spain.

Opportunities for women

During the Franco era, most Spanish women stayed at home to care for their children. Today, women make up nearly 40 percent of the working population and are able to work in many jobs and professions that were once only open to men. The legal status of Spanish women has also changed. Divorce was legalized in 1981, and family planning, previously forbidden by the Catholic Church, has been available since 1975.

Family ties

Although the picture of family life in Spain is changing, family ties remain strong and many traditional customs are still kept. Weddings, birthdays, and saints' days are important family occasions. Many city dwellers refer fondly to their *pueblo*—the town or village where their family comes from—and return home to visit whenever they can.

In rural areas, families are close-knit. Because so many seniors are cared for by their families, senior housing and nursing homes are rare in Spain.

▶ Falling birth-rates and rising life-expectancy mean that Spain now has a growing population of elderly people.

Religion and beliefs

For almost 500 years, Roman Catholicism was the official religion of Spain. Today, Catholicism is still the country's main religion, but only a minority of Spaniards go to church regularly. Currently, 79 percent of Spanish people describe themselves as Catholic, but only about a quarter of these attend church every week.

Church and state

Under Franco's rule, the Catholic Church and the government were closely linked. The government paid the salaries of priests, and until 1980, jobs in the Spanish civil service were only open to Roman Catholics.

A statue is carried in procession through the streets of a small Spanish town. Similar religious parades take place throughout the country during Easter week.

After Franco died, the influence of the church began to weaken. In 1977, Spain became a secular country and Catholicism ceased to be its official religion.

Other religions

As the influence of the Catholic Church has declined, other religions have become more widely practiced. With the recent influx of Muslim immigrants from North Africa, Islam has become the second-largest religion in Spain, with more than 1 million followers. Spain also has Protestant and Jewish communities, as well as Jehovah's Witnesses, Mormons, and Evangelical Christians.

Fiestas

In spite of the decline in churchgoing, religious festivals called *fiestas* still play a very big part in Spanish life. The main one is at Easter, when local clubs called *hermandades* or *cofradías* organize parades through the streets. Often, statues of saints or other religious figures are carried in procession.

One of the most popular fiestas is *Reyes*, or "kings." These are the three wise men who brought gifts to the infant Jesus in the Christian story of the Nativity. The Reyes bring Spanish children their Christmas presents on the night of Epiphany (January 6th).

⬀ The cathedral of Santiago de Compostela in Galicia, northern Spain, is visited by more than 100,000 Roman Catholic pilgrims every year. Many follow the traditional route traveled by pilgrims of the Middle Ages.

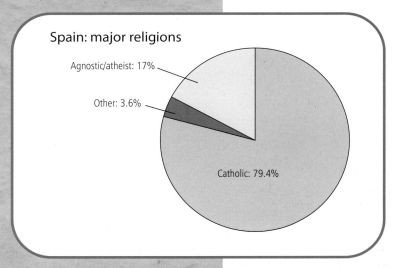

Spain: major religions

Agnostic/atheist: 17%
Other: 3.6%
Catholic: 79.4%

Education and learning

Before 1975, many of Spain's poor families could not afford to send their children to school. Today education is free and compulsory for all children 6 to 16 years old, and the state also provides free schooling for children from 3 to 5 years old.

A national system of education

Spain has a national curriculum, called the *Educación Secundaria Obligatoria* (ESO). The ESO lays down which subjects are compulsory—for example, math and science. Children are encouraged to take part in social activities, such as team sports and group projects. They must also study a foreign language. Most children choose to learn English and many also take private classes.

About a third of children in Spain go to private schools. Most of these are run by the Catholic Church. In state schools, students do not have to wear uniform, but private schools have strict rules about dress and behavior.

Crowded schools

Although schooling has improved in recent years, state schools in city centers often have large numbers of pupils from immigrant families who do not speak Spanish at home and who need extra help in class. Resources such as

Facts at a glance

Children in primary school: Male 100%; Female 99%

Children in secondary school: Male 97%; Female 100%

Adult literacy rate: Male 96.9%; Female 98.6%

▼ Students in Madrid prepare to take their college entrance exams.

computers are often in limited supply and in some regions, books have to be paid for by parents. In regions that have their own language, children have to learn two languages—for instance, Catalan and Spanish.

In primary schools, the day lasts from 9 a.m. until 5 p.m., including two hours for lunch and a *siesta*, or nap. Secondary schoolchildren have a *dia intensiva,* from 8.30 a.m. to 2.30 in the afternoon, with just a short mid-morning break. The school year is split into three terms and the school week is 30 hours long.

Higher education

At the age of 16, all children must take a set of national exams. If they pass, they can either stay at school or go to a technical college to learn a trade or profession. Students who stay at school take an exam called a *Bachillerato*. They can then take a university entrance exam, known as *Selectividad*.

⬤ Reading is not popular among Spanish children. But a worldwide phenomenon like the Harry Potter books helps children appreciate the magic of the written word.

DID YOU KNOW?
As well as Castilian Spanish, people in the Basque Country, Navarra, Catalonia, and Galicia have their own "official" language. Here, children have to learn both "Spanish" languages, as well as a "foreign" language!

Employment and economy

Until the 1960s, Spain was very poor compared to other European countries. The country's economy had suffered badly during the Civil War of 1936–39 and in the Franco era, when trade with the outside world was very limited. All this changed when the Spanish economy began to grow rapidly with the help of tourism, expansion of the service sector, and industrial development.

Tourism

Spain was one of the first countries to develop a large-scale tourist industry, and much of its wealth today is still based on tourism. Since the Olympic Games in Barcelona in 1992, tourist numbers have continued to rise. Spain is now the second most important tourist destination in the world after France. In 2006, the country earned a record $51.1 billion from tourism.

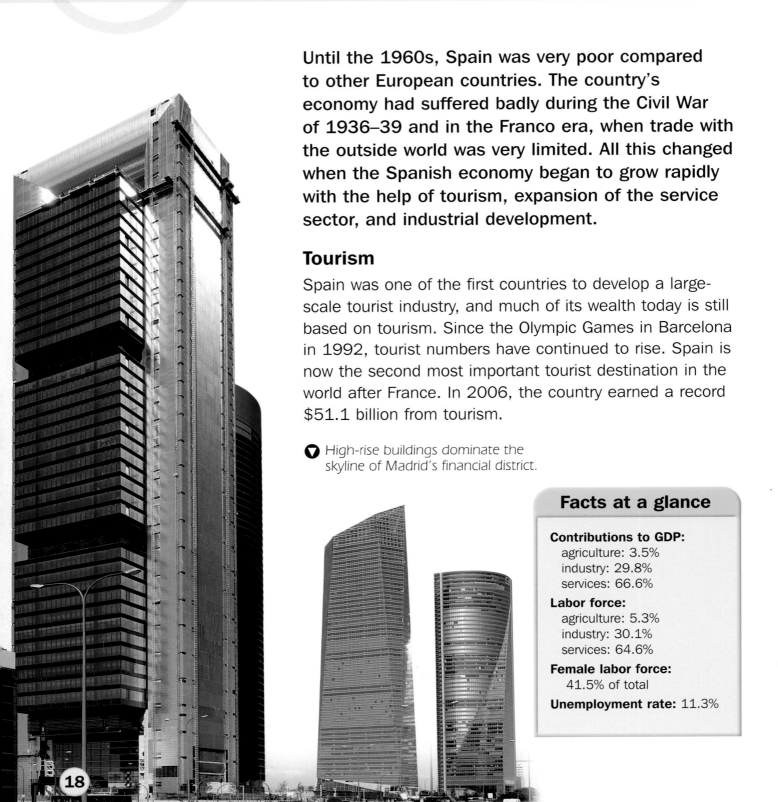

▼ High-rise buildings dominate the skyline of Madrid's financial district.

Facts at a glance

Contributions to GDP:
   agriculture: 3.5%
   industry: 29.8%
   services: 66.6%

Labor force:
   agriculture: 5.3%
   industry: 30.1%
   services: 64.6%

Female labor force:
   41.5% of total

Unemployment rate: 11.3%

A service economy

Although tourism has grown, however, other industries such as agriculture and fisheries have declined. From a mainly agricultural society, Spain has become a country dominated by service industries, and its economy relies heavily on revenue from abroad. Since 1986, when Spain joined the European Union (E.U.), more and more of its industries have been bought up by foreign investors looking for cheap local labor.

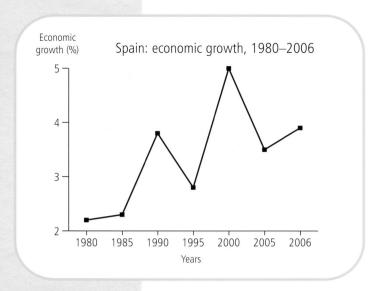

Spain: economic growth, 1980–2006

Unemployment

Although it continues to grow, the Spanish economy today is dependent on a narrow range of industries. Construction boomed as a result of the rise in the global property market, but has been badly hit by rising interest rates. Agriculture still provides many jobs, but these are mostly unskilled, low-paid, and seasonal.

Since 2004, many jobs in manufacturing have been lost as companies moved their factories from Spain to take advantage of lower costs in the new member countries of the E.U. The result is that unemployment is high in many key Spanish industries.

▼ Moroccan migrant workers on a farm in Andalusia.

DID YOU KNOW?

In Spain, many people try to avoid income tax by working for cash. *Dinero negro* ("black money") is also used to avoid tax on purchases. Some people even try to buy houses without telling the taxman.

Industry and trade

Although Spain imports large amounts of raw materials and goods from abroad, industries such as manufacturing, energy production, oil refining, chemical production, and food processing make a vital contribution to the Spanish economy.

Manufacturing

After Spain joined the E.U. in 1986, trade with other member countries increased and its industries grew rapidly. As foreign money flowed in, high-tech manufacturing began to replace more traditional heavy industries such as steelmaking.

Today, Spain's most important manufactured products are motor vehicles and domestic appliances such as refrigerators and washing machines. The country is also a world leader in solar energy and the manufacture of specialist products such as wind turbines.

DID YOU KNOW?
Spain is a world leader in solar power. At a vast site near Seville, Spanish scientists have developed the world's first solar thermal power plant. Mirrors concentrate the sun's rays, producing steam to drive a turbine.

▼ A wind farm in Andalusia. Alternative sources, such as wind, solar, and thermal power, are making a growing contribution to Spain's energy needs.

Heavy industry

In Spain, coal and iron are relatively scarce and of poor quality, and most of the traditional industries that use coal and iron are slowly disappearing. These are based in a region known as the "Rust Belt" in the north of the country.

Shipbuilding in Bilbao and La Coruña is helped by special grants and by a steady flow of work for the Spanish Navy. Keeping this industry alive is important, because it supports Spain's vast fishing fleet, the largest in the E.U.

Energy needs

Having virtually no fossil fuels, oil, gas, or coal of its own, Spain relies heavily on other countries for its energy needs. Most of the country's gas supply is imported from North Africa via a pipeline under the Mediterranean. From 2009, Spain will start importing electricity directly from France.

⬥ Goods manufactured in Spain wait to be loaded on board ships at Barcelona's giant container port.

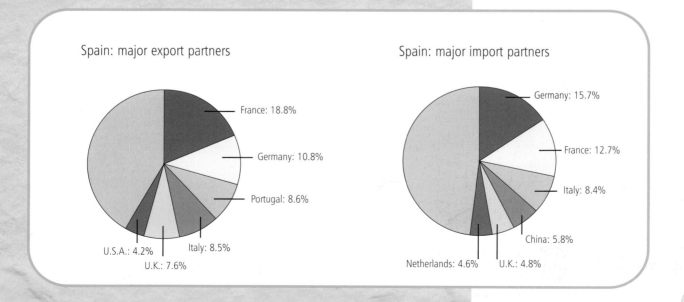

Spain: major export partners

- France: 18.8%
- Germany: 10.8%
- Portugal: 8.6%
- Italy: 8.5%
- U.K.: 7.6%
- U.S.A.: 4.2%

Spain: major import partners

- Germany: 15.7%
- France: 12.7%
- Italy: 8.4%
- China: 5.8%
- U.K.: 4.8%
- Netherlands: 4.6%

Farming and food

Although fewer Spanish people work on the land than in the past, Spain is still one of the leading agricultural producers in the E.U., and its fruit and vegetables are exported to countries all over northern Europe. Currently, it is the world's leading producer of olive oil and the third-largest producer of wine.

Farming methods

Over the last two decades, new methods have changed the face of Spanish farming. In parts of Andalusia in southern Spain, huge quantities of fruit and vegetables are grown in plastic polyethylene tunnels, called polytunnels. Although the soil is dry, the land is irrigated and crops can be grown all year round. Almost 25 percent of Spain's agricultural produce is now grown in this way.

Facts at a glance

Farmland: 37% of total land area

Main agricultural exports: Olive oil, wine, citrus fruits

Main agricultural imports: Beverages, prepared food

Average daily calorie intake: 3,410

A farmer irrigates a vineyard in Tarragona province, Catalonia.

Fishing

With almost 3,100 miles (5,000 km) of coastline, Spain has always had a big fishing industry. In the past, this provided the country with a plentiful supply of fish, but recently, overfishing has led to some species of fish dying out. Because of this, the E.U. has now limited the number of fish that can be caught. This means that many Spanish fishermen have had to look for jobs elsewhere.

△ Large-scale cultivation of crops in polytunnels and greenhouses has transformed the landscape of large areas of southern Spain.

Food and diet

Traditional foods such as fish, olives, bread, and wine are the main components of the Spanish diet, and help to keep Spanish people fit and healthy. The Spanish are especially proud of the variety of regional dishes. The most famous is *paella*, a Mediterranean rice dish made with seafood and chicken, traditionally served on Sundays and feast days. In the winter, people eat *fabada*, a dish of beans and pork that comes from Asturias in the far north.

DID YOU KNOW? Lunchtime in Spain can be as late as three o'clock in the afternoon, so Spaniards keep hunger at bay with *tapas* or snacks. These can be seafood, omelettes, salads, peppers, potatoes—and pigs' ears!

Transportation and communications

Spain's road and railroad networks radiate out from Madrid like the spokes of a wheel. Highways make it possible to reach all parts of the country from the capital, but the roads around the Mediterranean coast are heavily congested, and many rural roads in regions such as Galicia and Aragon are of poor quality.

Facts at a glance

Total roads: 414,015 miles (666,292 km)

Paved roads: 409,874 miles (659,629 km) [includes 7,462 miles (12,009 km) of highway]

Unpaved roads: 4,140 miles (6,663 km)

Railroads: 9,304 miles (14,974 km)

Total airports: 154

Major airports: 29

Ports: Algeciras, Barcelona, Bilbao, Cartagena, Huelva, Tarragona, Valencia

Railroads

Before railroads were built, mountain ranges made travel and transportation difficult within Spain. Nowadays, Spain has an excellent national railroad network linking all major towns and cities, and train travel is comfortable, reliable, and often cheaper than in many other E.U. countries. The new high-speed train network, called the *Alta Velocidad Española* (AVE) is transforming Spain's railroads and will link to France and the rest of Europe by 2011.

A network of fast highways connects Madrid with Spain's other major cities.

Urban transportation

Today, big urban centers like Madrid, Barcelona, and Bilbao all have good, affordable public transportation systems, with metros, local railroad networks, and trolley cars. To reduce pollution, cities have also improved commuter services, and on many roads, there are priority lanes reserved for cars carrying more than one passenger.

In Spain, factories and shopping malls are often built on the outskirts of cities, so workers and shoppers who live in the city center have to travel out, while people from the suburbs travel in to work. Fortunately, people work very different hours in Spain depending on the type of job they do. This helps to spread the demand for transportation and relieves congestion.

Telephone and Internet access

Modern telecommunications provided by the Spanish company Telefónica have transformed Spanish social life and business. Around 50 percent of Spanish homes now have Internet access. Cell phones are also on the increase. In remote parts of the country, there is often no cable telephone system, and cell phones are a vital communications link.

⬤ Like many Spanish cities, Bilbao now has good public transportation, including a trolley car system.

DID YOU KNOW? Spain's AVE trains are among the fastest and most reliable in the world. On the Madrid-Seville line, passengers receive a full refund if the train is more than 5 minutes late.

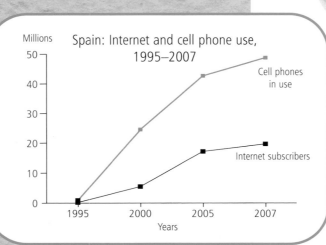

Millions

Spain: Internet and cell phone use, 1995–2007

Cell phones in use

Internet subscribers

Years

Leisure and tourism

Under Franco, entertainment, leisure, and the arts in Spain were all strictly controlled. Today, Spanish people are free to enjoy their leisure time in whatever way they choose.

Leisure and recreation

The *paseo*—a gentle afternoon or evening stroll with friends, neighbors, or family— is an important part of the Spanish daily routine. *Fiestas* are also hugely popular social events, bringing together all sections of the community and giving everyone a chance to celebrate their local culture and traditions.

Art and culture

Both pop and classical music are popular in Spain, and music by Spanish classical composers, such as Enrique Granados (1867–1916) and Isaac Albéniz (1860–1909), is widely performed.

Spanish literature is rich and varied, and many important works have been written in Spain's regional languages. Catalan literature is now flourishing after years of repression. Theater also suffered under Franco when plays were strictly censored, but is now becoming more popular with younger audiences.

Rooted in the folk culture of Andalusia, flamenco is a fiery blend of song, dance, and gypsy guitar rhythms.

Sports

One of Spain's most celebrated cultural activities is *La Corrida* or "the bullfight." The bull always dies, however, and the spectacle is brutal. Over half of Spaniards regard *La Corrida* as cruel and many are in favor of it being banned. The most popular spectator sport is soccer, and Spain's *La Liga* has some of the world's best teams, most notably Real Madrid and FC Barcelona.

Outdoor activities

Spain's wild and mountainous regions are ideal for adventure sports. Outdoor activities such as skiing, rock climbing, mountain-biking, caving, and paragliding have all grown in popularity, both with Spanish people and with visitors from abroad.

Tourism

Because of the scale and variety of the Spanish landscape, most Spanish people take their vacations in Spain rather than traveling abroad. Resort towns such as Santander on the northern coast are a popular destination for Spanish vacationers.

Facts at a glance

Tourist arrivals (millions)

Year	Arrivals
1995	34.9
2000	47.9
2005	55.9
2006	58.5

▶ Spectacular scenery and varied and colorful wildlife make hiking in the mountains one of Spain's most popular outdoor pursuits.

Environment and wildlife

With its large areas of wilderness, Spain has always been one of Europe's richest environments for wildlife. Wolves and brown bears can still be found in remote areas of the northeast of the country, and the wetlands around the deltas of the Ebro and Guadalquivir Rivers are among the most important places for migrating birds to pause on their long journeys between Europe and Africa.

Wildlife

Altogether, Spain has an estimated 630 species of animal and bird, of which 40 are endangered. To protect them, the country now has more than 400 nature reserves. These include 14 national parks where plants and wildlife are preserved and human activity that could endanger or harm them is banned.

DID YOU KNOW?
Spain is one of the last places in Europe where wolves still roam wild. In 2003, the wolf population was put at 2,000–2,500—the largest number anywhere outside Russia.

⊙ Situated in the heart of the Pyrenees, the Ordesa National Park is a haven for wild goats and many rare plant and animal species.

Despite the effects of overfishing, Spain's coastal waters still contain many varieties of fish and shellfish, especially in the south, where Atlantic and Mediterranean waters mix. Mammals such as the striped dolphin and the long-finned whale inhabit the waters off southeastern Spain, and the bottlenose dolphin is found off the Ebro delta.

Threats to wildlife

One of the most serious threats to Spain's wildlife is caused by the pesticides and fertilizers used by farmers. As well as poisoning birds, these chemicals kill the insects and grubs that other animals rely on for food.

New roads and the spread of cities also threaten wildlife by destroying habitats. Animals such as the European bear and Iberian lynx need space in order to breed successfully, and many habitats have been broken up by roads and railroad lines.

Greenhouse emissions

Spain's record on greenhouse emissions is poor. Between 1990 and 2004, emissions rose by more than 45 percent, making Spain one of the worst polluters in the E.U. More recently, the country has taken important steps to reduce its use of fossil fuels and switch to cleaner sources of energy.

In July 2008, the government approved plans to set up offshore wind parks along its coastline. Although more expensive than land-based farms, offshore wind parks are often more efficient, because they can take advantage of the stronger, steadier coastal breezes.

◔ This Eurasian is closely related to the Iberian lynx, which is the world's most threatened feline species and the most threatened carnivore in Europe.

Facts at a glance

Proportion of area protected: 8%

Biodiversity (known species): 5,697

Threatened species: 54

Carbon dioxide emissions: 304.9 million tons

Carbon dioxide emissions: 7.5 tons per capita

Glossary

Bachillerato exam that Spanish students take at the end of secondary school

biodiversity the different life forms that exist in a particular area

carnivore type of animal that eats other animals

censorship when books, movies, or other forms of expression are banned for political reasons

civil service workers and officials employed to run and maintain government offices

compulsory something that you must do

constitutional monarchy a country with a king or queen as head of state

drought a long period without rain

export good or service sold to another country

extended family different generations of the same family living close together and supporting one another

extremist person willing to break the law or use violence to achieve a political goal

family planning using contraception in order to avoid getting pregnant

fertilizer chemical substance to help crops grow

fossil fuel source of energy found below ground

GDP total value of goods and services produced by a country

habitat place where a person or an animal lives

immigration movement of people from one country to another

import good or service bought from another country

intensive farming using pesticides, fertilizers, and new technology to grow as much as possible on the land available

interest rate the cost of borrowing money from a bank or other lender

irrigation bringing water to a dry area in order to help grow crops

life expectancy average length of time people can expect to live

nationalist one who believes in putting the interests of their own country first

pesticide chemical substance that destroys animals or insects that feed on plants or crops

pilgrim someone who makes a special journey to visit a holy place or shrine

plateau a large, flat area of raised land

polytunnel polyethylene greenhouse tunnel used in intensive farming

population density average number of people living in an area

raw material resource such as timber and iron ore that is used to make products or other materials

republican one who supports democratic government and is opposed to monarchy or dictatorship

seasonal jobs that are only needed at certain times of the year

secular nonreligious. A secular country is one that does not have an official religion

Selectividad Spanish university or college entrance exam

service sector part of the economy that provides services such as banking, retail, education, and healthcare

sierra Spanish word for a mountain or mountain range

siesta Spanish word meaning rest or afternoon nap

Topic web

Use this topic web to explore Spanish
themes in different areas of study.

Geography
Make a list of the countries
that use Spanish as their
main language. Group the
countries into three main
geographical regions.
What do they have
in common?

Citizenship
Immigrants to Spain
come mainly from South
America, North Africa, and
Eastern Europe. Make
lists of the advantages
and disadvantages each
group may have in adapting
to life in Spain.

Science
Spain uses many
"renewable" sources for
generating electricity. Find
out how these sources
actually make electricity
and see what they all
have in common.

Maths
Calculate Spain's
population density by
dividing its area by the
population. Repeat this for
each of Spain's regions,
and list each one in order
from highest to lowest.

Spain

History
Find out about the two
sides in the Spanish Civil
War (1936–9). Which side
won and what happened to
the losing side?

English
Imagine that you have a
Spanish "pen pal." Write a
letter that describes three
ways in which your daily life
may differ from his or hers,
and three ways in which
they may be the same.

**Information
Technology**
Use the Internet to find out
about Spain's autonomous
regions. Include capital city,
area, population, rainfall,
and average temperature.
Make a "fact file" of each
region and illustrate it
to show how each
one is unique.

**Design and
Technology**
One of Spain's major
products, olive oil, is made
by squeezing olives to
extract the oil. Design a
press that would do this.
Don't forget to include a
way of collecting the oil!

Further Information, Web Sites, and Index

Further reading

Countries of the World: Spain by Neil Champion (Facts on File, 2005)
Country Files: Spain by Ian Graham (Smart Apple Media, 2003)
Looking at Spain by Jillian Powell (Gareth Stevens Publishing, 2007)

Web Sites

Due to the changing nature of Internet links, PowerKids Press has developed an online list of Web sites related to the subject of this book. This site is updated regularly. Please use this link to access this list:
http://www.powerkidslinks.com/discovc/spain/

Index